# Praise for Transformational Healing

In her book *Transformational Healing: Shifting Into an Uplifting Perspective*, Alejandria Kate shines a light on the shadows of her own life and openly shares the wonderful masterpiece that awaits us all when we really see ourselves. With the grace and authenticity of a true teacher, she guides readers to a healthier understanding of themselves through exercises that cause us to dig deep, which is where true transformation occurs, in the depths. I LOVE the truth and the message of this book. It's a must-read!

Sunny Dawn Johnston, Best-selling Author, Teacher and Psychic Medium
www.sunnydawnjohnston.com

For anyone who has ever said, life should come with an owner's manual – now it does! Alejandria's book begins by allowing the reader into her own world of personal struggles and then guides them through the techniques she developed to help her not only to survive, but to thrive and grow beyond limitations. It shows us not only what triggers our fears, but how our love can heal them. This is a workbook that can transform your life!

Gerry Gavin, Best-selling Author of *Messages from Margaret*, and *If You Could Talk to an Angel* www.gerrygavin.com

*Transformational Healing: Shifting Into an Uplifting Perspective* by Alejandria Kate is beautifully written and timelessly poignant, as it retraces the steps of a journey that no one wants to take. We don't always get to choose what happens in this life, but we can choose to grow in compassion and wisdom as a result.

The majesty of love radiates from every page of this powerful book as we follow Alejandria's soul journey. In this frank and personal account of her life so far, we witness the transformation from the darkness of despair to true spiritual enlightenment.

Reading this heartfelt, wise, and tender account expressed through Alejandria's gentle voice as a writer, we are privileged to share personal yet memorable life lessons and poignant anecdotes.

The underlying message is one of hope and healing, for the true art of spiritual living is the ability to use misfortune in a constructive fashion. Alejandria Kate has provided a first-class example of how this can be accomplished. She shares with us the gift of awareness and the grace of love. Every word rings with truth, kindness, and the beauty of the human spirit.

We can't fail to be moved by this book. It is a valuable companion filled with spiritual insights and a book unlike anything I have ever read. It is an offering from a true spiritual friend. *Transformational Healing: Shifting Into an Uplifting Perspective* is sure to serve as support and inspiration for many.

A warm and glowing book to be treasured!

Maire Davies, Spiritualist Medium
www.mairedavies.com

# Transformational Healing

## Shifting Into an Uplifting Perspective

## Alejandria Kate

TRANSFORMATIONAL HEALING

Shifting Into an Uplifting Perspective

By Alejandria Kate

Copyright © 2018 Alejandria Kate

All rights reserved.

No part of this publication may be reproduced, distributed, or transmitted in any form or by any means, including photocopying, recording, or other electronic or mechanical methods, without the prior written permission of the publisher, except in the case of brief quotations embodied in critical reviews and certain other noncommercial uses permitted by copyright law.

Generally Verbose
www.alejandriakate.com

ISBN-13: 978-0-578-41926-8

Printed in the United States of America.

# Dedication

Eternal appreciation to my father, for teaching me that our imperfections cannot obfuscate a good heart; to my mother, for showing me how to continue in love while embracing change; to my brother, for being a safe haven and teaching me trust; to my sister, for showing me the grace in forgiveness; to Andy Byng, for teaching me the healing power of spiritual meditation and mediumistic, personal development; to Sunny Dawn Johnston, for opening the door to self-love and raising the bar to the kind of woman I aspired to become; to my friends, for walking in the Light alongside me, and to everyone who has ever broken my heart and betrayed me, for showing me the strength of my soul and for helping me find the Light within myself. Last but not least, for the people I may have hurt while on my healing journey, I am truly sorry.

# Contents

Foreword ..................................................................................... i

Author Preface ........................................................................... v

The Golden Road Within ......................................................... 1

Window of Perception ............................................................. 7

Lava-Lava Love ...................................................................... 11

The Emotion Wheel ............................................................... 15

Life Is Our Healer .................................................................. 19

Exercise .................................................................................. 23

Into the Integration ............................................................. 135

The Dark Side of the Lily .................................................... 139

You Are the Creator ............................................................ 143

Joyful Creation .................................................................... 147

Personal Note from Author ................................................ 157

About the Author ................................................................ 161

"Everything we're searching for is within us."

# Foreword

Grief, in all its forms – whether it is the loss of a loved one, a job, a home, a family, or a sense of self – is perhaps the most challenging experience we can encounter as human beings. The problem with grief is that it not only affects us in those moments that we are conscious of it, but it can linger and adversely influence us both subconsciously and unconsciously. As such, there may be moments when the choices that we make, the way we interact with people, and the way in which we perceive the experiences we have, are being influenced by a grief that we are not even conscious of. As we are not conscious of it, the reason why we act the way we do, the reason why we make the choices we make, and the reason why we feel the way we feel about ourselves, may forever remain a mystery to us, evading us at every turn.

Indeed, we often put the cause of our suffering down to an entirely different reason, or merely accept that it is just the way we are, or that this is the way life is, and never, therefore, uncover, accept and understand the grief that is the true cause of our suffering.

If we are to create a positive change within ourselves, and thus our lives, we must uncover, understand and accept the experiences that are the cause of our grief. Ironically, it is our choices that often create grief within our life, and so a vicious circle can often be formed in which our choices, rooted in subconscious or unconscious grief, create new and more complex forms of grief: grief, therefore, begets grief.

My work as a Spiritualist Medium, has not only led me on a personal spiritual journey of self-discovery, but it has afforded me the privilege of helping people come to terms with their own grief. While mediumship has taught me so much about life, and the nature of the human condition, its real gift has been to reveal to me the knowledge that change does not come from looking outwardly, but rather by looking inwards: it begins and ends with the Self. It is only when we begin to explore the interior, spiritual, world of the soul – when we climb the lofty heights of our intellect, and mine the depths of our emotions – that we begin to forge an honest and open relationship with our soul. A relationship within which we can acknowledge and celebrate our positive attributes and talents, but are also willing to understand, through our emotions, those experiences and facets of our self that affect us in more adverse ways.

I first met Alejandria Kate in 2016, during a seminar on mediumistic and personal development, where I taught her, amongst other things, a spiritual meditation practice. Since then, I have witnessed Alejandria – through the practice of meditation and mediumistic development, as well as her own personal practices – embark on a personal spiritual journey.

The culmination of Alejandria's journey thus far is her inspirational workbook *Transformational Healing: Shifting Into an Uplifting Perspective.* The book itself encourages the reader to turn inwardly, and helps us to understand and navigate the important relationship between our internal and external lives. *Transformational Healing* places emphasis on mindfulness and reflection as a means to understand the Self. By doing so it encourages the reader to release and confront the grief that is consciously, subconsciously or unconsciously affecting them, so that they may transcend their grief and create positive change within their life. It aims at doing this through a constructive and beneficial exercise that is rooted in self-reflection and self-expression, with the overall aim of breaking the viscous cycle of grief begetting grief.

Alejandria's natural positivity and tenacity shines through in her book, and her courage in divulging details of her own childhood demonstrates the degree to which she has accepted and healed from the very experiences that were the root of her own grief and suffering.

I have always believed that spiritual teachers ought to only teach what they themselves have experienced. This personal spiritual journey, which is open to every one of us, is one that has to be rooted in personal experience. Each part of the journey can only be understood and intellectualized once it has been experienced. It is this personal experience, which forms the basis of Alejandria's work, that gives her book *Transformational Healing* the authenticity that it requires. A workbook that I am sure will aide many in their quest of transformation.

Andy Byng, Spiritualist Medium

www.andybyng.com

# Author Preface

There was a time when I believed I would never find the Light within me. Life felt hopeless, and it was as if I had fallen into a black hole within myself. Oftentimes, I would get in my car at night and speed along the highway, screaming and crying as I tried to purge the pain within me. Other times, I longed for death, anything to escape a world that seemed devoid of beauty.

I no longer feel this way, but the journey has been by no means easy. I had a boatload of pain to wade through – grief; heartbreak; violence; sexual assault; sexual abuse; murder; betrayal; disrespect and emotional abuse. I have known it all. As a child, I knew what it felt like to have to bark for my food and eat it off the floor.

My childhood was a confusing mixture of beautiful love and emotionally damaging abuse. My father would give the clothes off his back to help other people. He was a hard worker, and I never went hungry. In so many ways he was supportive of me, proud of me, and protective of my safety.

> "All of our painful experiences bring out our greatest strength. Our deep love is the brightest LIGHT in the darkness. Following the love in any 'dark' situation is like following the light out of a cave and into a bright day."

But he was also a violent alcoholic, and his personal demons – stemming from unresolved emotional trauma – created an instability that affected every aspect of his life and the lives of those closest to him. This emotionally tortured

> "Your strength lies in your love. The journey of humanity is not a straight one, but all roads end in the Light. The road less traveled is the most difficult road. Yet, it's the straightest of all. That road is a road of love. Choose wisely."

human being brought both Light and darkness onto my path. The moments of Light were brilliant, but the heavy moments, when he was intoxicated, were devastating.

The dysfunctional combination was not an easy road to walk, and it created great emotional hurdles I've had to jump through within myself. It also, however, afforded me an incredible opportunity. It challenged my soul to step up and embrace love over hate. It taught me to see beyond others' negative behavior and explore the emotional pain fueling their actions. I learned compassion toward humanity and gained personal resolutions in the gift of the experience.

Each painful experience allowed my heart to expand, and made me more beautiful inside. What I perceived as grievances against me were actually healing opportunities. Every horrifying experience cracked my soul open to feel more, to love deeper. The pain became a shovel, unearthing the greatest love within myself.

My first spiritual experience was in my late teens, after the murder of my aunt and her two children. It was while in the grips of extreme grief that I saw my beloved aunt, standing in spirit next to my bed! She was beckoning me to notice a spiritual doorway that had always been open for me. At once awestruck and afraid, I would keep the sighting a secret for many years.

My next glimpse into the spiritual realm occurred after my father passed away. Synchronistic events started occurring, such as the numbers 808, appearing to me regularly and in different forms – for example, I'd wake up at 8:08 a.m., receipts would add up to $8.08 and so on.

# AUTHOR PREFACE

It happened so often my friends and family even started to take notice. Though I didn't know what to make of these synchronistic experiences, I did not feel fearful. Rather, I felt supported and the presence of great love. Moreover, I was becoming aware that something beautiful (though I didn't know what) existed beyond the physical dimension I was standing in. This evolution from faith to a knowing was the start of my personal healing journey.

I started reading books that helped me to understand my mind and my emotions. I read books that challenged my old perceptions. I started therapy and over time watched countless sunsets, searching for beauty to hold onto. I learned to forgive others, forgive myself, and, eventually, embraced the gifts in each experience.

> "Every obstacle, every challenge, every person, is an opportunity to help us evolve into the individual we need to be in order to accomplish what we set out to do before we came into this incarnation. Our challenging experiences deliver spiritual tools that build a staircase to everything. A change in perception equates to gratefulness."

In 2014, another family member violently lost her life, and it hurt so badly all I could do was cry and rock myself back and forth. When this failed to comfort me, I fell to my knees and begged God to hold me. I often thought of taking my own life, and might have, if not for the devastation it would have caused my mother.

I'd never been so scared, and I felt a thickness in the energy around me. I prayed and pushed the white Light of my soul up and out of me, and I saw a beautiful violet Light enveloping the room. I then had a distinctive feeling, a knowing to breathe in the violet Light, and blend the Light of my soul with the Light around me.

In that moment of surrender, I saw blue and white twinkling Lights and what appeared like the Universe opening up above me. It was like my room had transformed into a cosmic realm, and the brightest white Light filled up the space around me.

For several years, beautiful white Lights would "float" down around me and purple smoky-looking Light would fill up my room. The violet Light "moved" in a breathing motion, fading in, fading out. Words are inadequate to describe it, but it was as if the Universe was *breathing* with me, keeping me alive.

I would spend hours in the quiet, watching the Light(s), and speaking out loud to this invisible world. It was the start of a spiritual journey, an adventure within myself that led me, finally, to resolve the abuse that had haunted me for years.

During my spiritual healing journey, inspired writing entered my life. I started putting pen to paper and beautiful wisdom channeled through guiding me to the Light within myself and reminding me that love is a healer. The quotes and writings in this workbook are a few of my spiritually inspired gems.

Following the trail of my emotions and allowing myself to feel the pain in each experience, I've let the pain in life teach me. I've learned about who I am. I have realized the strength of my character and the power of my love. Every challenge has left me more understanding and kind to myself and others. I've learned discernment and how to care for myself. Experiencing adversity advanced my soul. I found beauty in the pain.

It took a long time to get to a place of inner peace, but these days I trust that experiences unfold the way they're supposed to and adversity in life is an avenue that helps us grow spiritually. I'm thankful for the hurt because it inspired growth of my soul in ways beneficial to me.

# AUTHOR PREFACE

There is a bigger picture than we can see. We are spiritual beings having a human experience. Wading through the illusions and rising to the Light within is our birthright; it's our mission.

I choose to focus on the energy of love. This has brought inner peace, happiness, and helps me navigate through the hard times that are inevitable.

It is my hope that a smile, a loving word, and/or a kind gesture can make a difference to another human being. Am I perfect? No, and I still have my difficult moments, but now I have tools to build bridges instead of walls within myself.

We do not know the pain other people have experienced or are currently experiencing in their lives. Hurtful events in our lives may feel personal, but in detachment there is grace. This world is a realm of learning.

We can help one another through kindness. One kind word can give someone the strength to make it through the darkness. Never underestimate the power of love.

Life is a winding road, with challenges and opportunities, storms and sunny days around every bend. We cannot always control the events happening around us, but if we walk the road, knowing it's going to be a challenge and are still willing to charge ahead, we will be rewarded with bountiful opportunities to become wiser, more centered, and more compassionate. We will have the opportunity to rediscover our authentic selves.

> "Flow with what feels natural and allow beauty to come in and out of your life. Every experience is beauty recreating itself. The issue is in the judgment of the experience, the control of the outcome, the creation of unhappiness."

After my father passed away he visited me in a dream. We were sitting on a park bench and I asked him, "Why do I have to stay here? It hurts too much."

"Because," he replied, "life is beautiful."

Life *is* beautiful; however, its beauty lies not in perfection, but in its ability to help us perfect ourselves. This is a continuous and ever-evolving process.

The term evolve is derived from the Latin word *ēvolvere*, which means "to unroll." Within this word are the verb love spelled backward and the adverb vere, meaning "truly." Moving out of the darkness into the Light requires a shift of position, a shift in perspective. Perhaps, then, our lives are a beautiful evolutionary process of a gradual opening up and unfoldment to the ultimate gift: true love within our Universal selves.

Emotional storms are unavoidable, so is pain. Embrace every experience. Let life teach you, evolve you, and grace you with its love. For life is our healer and within life are gifts of grief.

> "No matter the love you feel toward another person, it doesn't mean they have all the answers. Turn within and listen to your own soul's language, the spark of intuition, your soul's wisdom to guide you. Learn to identify what intuition feels like. This is the first step in listening and trusting the wisdom of your own soul."

"Make choices that light up your path."

# The Golden Road Within

In life, we often get caught up in our own pain. Like soldiers in a war-torn land, we go through our days on high alert and in survival mode. We build walls to protect our hearts from dangers, and are often so intent on manning those walls that we don't recognize the love trying to penetrate them. We also miss beautiful and often subtle opportunities to be of service to others.

Love is the road upon which we can venture out of our individualized prisons and into the world. Everyone has their own story, their own fears, and an inner torment that hounds them every day. If we can separate from attachments and find freedom in the great peace within, we will discover that inner serenity is the greatest love we can know.

We tend to take things personally (it certainly *feels* personal when someone hurts us). However, in reality, another's actions have little to do with us, and everything to do with his/her private journey. We can serve another better by trying to understand them, by slowing down our knee-jerk responses and speeding up our extension of love and kindness. Start seeing others through their pain. You'll find compassion rises to the top, like cream.

Nature has so much wisdom to offer us. Long before we see the radiant bloom of the flower, the seed must first be dropped into the darkness. From the help of the elements, and ultimately, the power of self, the seed breaks through its hard shell and blends with the soil around it before rising to the light.

Part of the human journey into a spiritual awakening is spent walking in the darkness. But is it really darkness being unearthed within us, or Light? Healing can be a painful process, but new growth prevails. Many of us have been hurt and wounded. A journey inward on the golden road brings forth a Lightness of being, a love for mankind, and a glory and appreciation for one's self that outshines the chaos.

> "People grow. People change. The love of Spirit is nourishment to the soul. Celebrate one another's progress. If one feels the need to continually label another's character based on an outdated personality, perhaps look within and understand one's own desire in pursuing harshness."

The golden road within isn't easy and requires a commitment that only the journeyman can live up to. There will be challenges that bring one to their knees and tears that bathe the soul. But the sunrise and sunsets of each day give life to our heart's ever-expansion.

Letting go of attachments is a golden key of awareness. Contrary to what many believe, we don't own anyone. Families are gifts. Spouses are gifts. Our friends and every person in every situation, no matter how painful, are gifts.

Some gifts float into our lives like beautiful dandelions, softly touching our lives. Other experiences roar and shake us up a little bit. *All* experiences serve us. Trusting and surrendering into the gift sends out waves of gratitude. Everything moves us along.

When we own our choices, our mistakes, and our misgivings, we realize that the people in our lives are simply other journeymen finding their own way on the golden road within. They do not, as we might have felt, have any true power over us, just the power we grant them. The sooner we let these attachments go, the brighter our road becomes.

As travelers on the golden road, perhaps we should focus on the Light within and outside us, embrace how expansive that Light is, and know that there is enough for everyone. Let go of our attachments and desires to consume. By clinging, we can inadvertently bring more pain into another's life, keeping a cycle of dormancy that serves no one.

Trust in the Light and make space for others to walk their golden road separately, each of us in our own Light. But we are *One*, and on a singular journey to the same place.

If we don't own people but only own our choices, what are we?

Perhaps we're the sunlight on a dewy morning leaf, or the cry in a newborn's wail, or the buzzing of the hummingbird's wings. Maybe we're everything that breathes and everything that cries, and in that knowledge is the power we all have: the power of love, and the knowing that we're all *One*. In that knowing, love bubbles up to help us rise.

Be the Light and walk in the Light. Love with all your heart. And when life knocks you down, bow your head to the soil, plant more seeds, and rise in love.

"You're a spiritual being on a human journey. There are supposed to be challenges. So instead of despairing during moments of difficulty, learn to breathe with the Universe. This life is like a breath. It has a flow. Even the waves have a flow. And sometimes the moon causes bigger, crashing waves and then there is stillness. Life knocks us around and it does this because it's supposed to. It's a natural rhythm aimed to nourish and enliven. If one is open to the possibility, the journey to inner stillness becomes an adventure. Difficulties become diamonds. Take a chance and breathe with the Universe."

"One's perception colors what is seen."

# Window of Perception

Developing as a person is amazing, challenging and, at times, painful. It's certainly a lifelong treasure. It's a lot of realizations that arrive one by one.

Finding the quiet within and listening to the wisdom of our own soul invites a fresh perception, and the layers of our current awareness peel in a different direction. It's like a mirror comes up each time, and if we follow the inner road, all signs point to us, our reactions and defenses, and what we create based on the tools we have in that moment.

Recognizing our own walls, acknowledging how we created them, and smashing them down creates new tools to advance further as people, as personalities, as souls – tools that build roads instead of walls within us.

We make things about us because of hidden pain, and our reactions are a key to the healing needed within us. It's not about external circumstances and other people; it's about what's within us. Yes, experiences are sometimes out of our control and others hurt us, but the residual imprint of pain is a cause and

> "You may not be understood. Perhaps someone will mock and ridicule your sensitive heart, your kindness and your forgiving nature. Love anyway. Being loving and compassionate is not about other people nor is it about receiving anything back. It's about being true to who you are and appreciating and unfolding the best part of yourself."

effect, and discovering internal walls is our healing process. And through this healing we embrace our power; the great love within our soul. Self-love is the root that feeds the flower of our personal growth.

Adversity is the gift to unfold the petals of our soul. It's through adversity that we learn discernment, responsibility and reverence in our own imperfection through our unhealed pain.

There is beauty to be found in our own self-created chaos, our painful experiences with others and life's imperfection.

> "The word 'Devil' is the word 'lived' spelled backward. Perhaps, then, the Devil is not some discarnate being attacking, tempting and haunting us, but merely a word for the challenges one lives. Maybe one gives too much credence to an outside force when the Devil is simply the suffering involved in being alive. Does one allow the storms of life to dim the inner Light or does one rise above the darkness and into the Light? This is the individual choice of free will. The Devil is the self-illusions in a life lived. It is the journey of overcoming inner obstacles set up to develop spiritual power, knowledge and enlightenment. Live each day as an opportunity to raise your vibration. Dissolve the illusions and create your own path.
> Live a life in the Light, a life well lived."

"Reach for the light in another and rise to your own light."

# Lava-Lava Love

Anger. It's a perfectly natural human emotion, so why are we so afraid of it? Why do we go to such lengths to avoid others' anger and hide our own?

We put barriers on our lives that do not serve us. One way is by judging our emotions. Anger is as much a part of life as feelings of joy or sadness, the feelings of fear or falling in love, so rather than labeling it as a negative, our energy may be better spent finding a healthy outlet for it.

I make an effort to meditate every day, and oftentimes Spirit provides me with visuals that provide clarity and truth. In one such meditation I saw two of my spirit guides standing with me. I don't see faces in my meditations; I see beings of Light and I hear words of wisdom. They conveyed to me that anger is a natural human emotion. They showed me an image of a volcano. A volcano is made to release its lava. That's what it does. There is another kernel of wisdom here as well: perhaps if we release the lava of our anger slowly and we explore the anger as it arises, we can avoid a devastating eruption later on.

> "Sometimes the best gifts come through the most hurtful experiences. It's the unwrapping of the gift that's the hardest part of receiving."

> "All emotions have a purpose. Each is a teacher and will reveal what needs to be healed within. When healing occurs it is in the detachment that a blending takes place. Like colors, alone they have a purpose, a meaning, but, when blended, they become one in the purity of love."

In my meditation, I saw red-hot lava flowing out of my mouth and into the center of the earth. No one was hurt, and, afterward, I felt a release within me. Maybe the answer is to feel our anger, rather than run from it. Perhaps the way to deal with anger is like applying Kleenex to a teardrop. You just deal with it softly.

If something happens that invites anger into our lives it's something to explore, honor and then release. Like every other human emotion, it's there to serve us and teach us and sometimes protect us, so let it be there and breathe into it. Maybe anger is a form of self-love, an intuitive spark within us saying: Hey, I deserve better.

Now, when I'm angry, I look for healthy ways to release the feelings. I have a journal in which I write down my thoughts, and sometimes I burn the pages to release the energy. Sometimes I drive in my car alone and let the anger out, my favorite curse words flying left and right. Remember, the only person who truly punishes you for being angry, is you.

Within anger, there is insight, wisdom, growth, and love to be unfolded.

"The storm inside is the pathway for nourishment and growth of the soul. Dig deep into the soil of truth and grow roots into the Divine."

**Emotion Wheel Diagram**

# The Emotion Wheel

Emotions are our heart's voice; they comprise a cosmic language of expression guiding us to healing. In place of judgment, embrace the inner emotional oracle – a compass and guidepost to soul healing.

The emotion wheel diagram is available to assist the reader in identifying specific emotions. Having clarity into one's inner emotional world assists in the movement of emotion(s) and a release of the stagnant energy attached to an experience.

> "Start observing personal relationships and how they are playing out. The matter of unfinished emotional chaos within is reenacted via the roles people play in life. Until the personal reaction changes and progression succeeds, the roles cannot shift. The same act plays itself out in different people but the same subconscious role. Anything that is a struggle is a map to healing within the one experiencing pain."

"We're the candle and our soul is a flame of Light...

...Create beauty out of the shadows."

# Life Is Our Healer

We are navigating a world of perfect imperfection. Like a snake that sheds its skin and makes a sideways-forward journey, we're constantly evolving, and there's going to be rocks, storms, and other catastrophes along the curvy road. It's the little detours that help us spiritually by providing the opportunity to learn, to go within, and break through barriers.

Each barrier conquered is like a shedding of the skin, a rising of vibration, and a moving forward in new growth. It is the constant expectation – and our attachment to it – that causes us pain and slows the process.

Let life be the healer. Like a flower, unfold to the Light of Source for Spirit is like water washing over and blessing us. And the hellish fires disguised as life's adversity are designed to tear us down for a rebirth of continuous beauty. The seed of the soul cannot be destroyed.

> "Processing feelings after a hurtful experience may take time. Getting from the head into the heart can be like fruit ripening on a branch. Ground yourself, sway in the wind, and, in its own time, allow the flower of your soul to ripen in the sweetness of love."

Perhaps our individual purpose is simply the evolution of perfection within ourselves, and life, our greatest healer, is rising to the occasion and lending a hand.

"Use life experiences to your benefit. Let the dark experiences become like ink and write a new chapter...

...Make it a love story."

"Live courageously in this world. All experiences are an opportunity for learning. Falls are a part of the journey. The fall shows beauty at another level. Within this space there is opportunity. Difficulty affords building of character and expansion of the soul. Light is within; illuminate and behold the beauty in the imperfection of life and what it is teaching. Remember perfection is within the soul. The soul is Light. There are no mistakes. There is no death, only regrowth, recreation and a rising of love."

# Exercise

Exploring how we perceive certain words and phrases can be a window into one's inner conflict and a road to self-healing. A change in perception opens up inner doorways.

Perception goes a long way in either helping us grow in our development or pulling us down into our own darkness. The mind is a powerful tool. Yet, it can shade the heart from the Light.

The following pages offer the opportunity to look within our own perceptions of certain words and phrases. These words and phrases are perceptual doorways into our own reactions. Some of those perceptions may be negative and not serving us. Perhaps it's time to let go of an old way of thinking and create a new thought process that serves our forward expansion.

Please take your time and explore how each word and/or phrase feels to you. Explore how this word and/or phrase has integrated into the psyche and the emotional facets of your being.

Healing is a journey in itself, so take the time to let the flower within you unfold its petals to the Light that you are and always have been.

## Instructions:

Words and phrases are included in this workbook for personal exploration. Some of these words and/or phrases signify universal fears of events or phobias. Other words/phrases may elicit an emotional trigger based in personal trauma.

Peruse the list and start with the word/phrase that evokes the strongest emotion. Continue forward in the same manner with each word/phrase. Consider how each word/phrase feels in your mind, in your body, in your emotions, and how this word has played out in your life.

If you think of a word that is not on the list, add it to the list. Remember this is your healing space and personal to you.

What does the word/phrase mean to you?

Expressing what the word/phrase personally means to the reader is the first step. Don't hold back.

Does it make you angry? Do you feel uncomfortable? Why? What attachments do you have to each word/phrase? Do the feelings attached to this word/phrase bring peace or is emotional turmoil swirling around in you?

Even if you need to unleash rage, pain and soak the page with tears, write out exactly your definition of each word/phrase. Share on paper what feelings the word/phrase unravels in you. You may be surprised what comes onto the paper. Do not judge it. Allow the emotions to come alive, breathe, and show you what it truly is.

Also, do not edit yourself in content or in length. This workbook has space to explore 20 emotional doorways, but don't stop there.

If you need more space, attach additional pages to the workbook and allow yourself to express as much as is needed.

Dive deep into the vortex of chaos inside of you, knowing that you set aside this time and place for your personal healing journey, and that each step brings you closer to healing and the Light within you.

Should a word/phrase elicit a mild reaction and you find yourself on the fence considering if there's need for emotional exploration, highlight the word/phrase and revisit it. Sometimes we have to peel back the layers of an emotion to find and understand subconscious blocks.

After you have expressed yourself completely, read what you've written. Sit with it and feel how it feels.

Do you feel relieved? Are you surprised what has come onto the paper?

The next step is exploring the emotional havoc created by the experiences attached to each word/phrase.

Do you recognize that there are negative attachments to these various words/phrases? Are you becoming aware of how these attachments are negatively affecting your way of thinking, affecting your inner peace, and affecting your ability to move forward with a positive mindset and an open heart?

Are you exhibiting controlling behavior or obsessive behavior rooted in fear that these words and/or phrases bring up for you?

Is your old way of thinking progressing or hindering you? How exactly is this frame of mind affecting your emotions? How are these emotions affecting your life? Has it held you back in pursuing joy? Do you feel fearful in taking chances?

Recognizing negative perceptions is the first step.

The next step is finding the pearl in the experience. How did your soul grow? What lessons were learned? Did the experience make you more compassionate?

Find the positive in the experience. Even painful experiences teach us, refine us, and they build character.

Now, the last page is for a new beginning. This is where we create a new direction mentally and emotionally. Our perception needs a makeover.

You now recognize the spiritual gifts in the experience, the strength of character that ensued due to the experience, and the responsibility of self in any negative perception. It is time to let go of an old way of thinking and create a more positive belief system based on a new perception of each word and/or phrase.

Why hold on to that which only offers inner chaos and negativity? Would we consciously travel down dead-end roads, or would we prefer a road surrounded by scenery that provides continuous positive adventure?

It is now time to evolve the prior negative belief system attached to these words and/or phrases into a positive frame of reference.

This practical hands-on portion of the workbook will help explore the chaos inside mental perceptions. It is also an opportunity to discover emotional triggers that lie beneath the surface of your experiences; triggers that hijack your emotional wellbeing.

This is your time, your space and your healing. Enjoy the adventure, the inner journey, and trust where this experience can take you within yourself.

As spiritual beings on a human journey, matters of the human state are simply avenues to growth of the soul. Words, phrases, experiences, only have the power we give them. Follow the inner chaos, create a new perception, and open a doorway to personal growth.

Part of healing is discovering how we're giving our power away. Illusions appear real and in detachment, there is a sacred gateway to love and healing.

Are you ready? Let's do this!

**Potentially emotionally charged words and phrases are listed on the following pages. Take a deep breath and trust that exploring the pain of an outdated belief system is exactly what your soul needs for healing.**

## Peruse the following words and phrases. Circle the words and/or phrases that elicit the strongest reaction.

| | | |
|---|---|---|
| Money | Crazy/mad | Unwanted |
| Religion | Spontaneous | Loyalty |
| Debt | Disrespect | Dishonor |
| Ugly | Mother/mom/mum/ | Incest |
| Home ownership | stepmother/adoptive | Ridiculous |
| Crying | mother | Weird |
| Adversity | Father/dad/stepfather/ | No-strings-attached |
| Abortion | adoptive father | "Grow some balls" |
| Birth control | Exposed | Trauma |
| Trust | Forbidden | Moist |
| Fragile | Sex | Power |
| Dirty | Infidelity/cheater | Conditional |
| Joy | Spiders | Bipolar |
| Change | Never | "You're wrong" |
| Invasion | Friendship | Death/dead/dying |
| Boring | Fraud | Light |
| Expectation | Raw | Ethnicity |
| Pathetic | Lover | Secret |
| Education | Wrong | Health |
| Pregnant | Sexual abuse | Confined space |
| Stability | Positive thinking | Snakes |
| Inferior | Silence | Want |
| Guilt | Slavery | Daft |
| Perfect | Prostitution | Shy |
| Sadist | Integrity | Belittling |
| Marriage | Pig | Unworthy |
| Ignorant | Falling | Hope |
| Occupation | Pain | Broken |
| Asshole | Unmarried | Divine |
| Phony | Worthy | "You people" |
| Flirting | Boyfriend | Bondage |
| Passion | Mistake | Absurd |
| Drama | Girlfriend | Heaven |
| Apology/"I'm sorry" | Mask | Relax |
| Risk/risky | Failure | Single parenthood |

EXERCISE

| | | |
|---|---|---|
| Pornography | Embarrassed | Shatter |
| Truth | Bank account balance | Too sensitive |
| Miscarriage | Morbid | I understand how you feel |
| Infertility | Illegal | Automobile make/model |
| Boss/manager | Disgusting | Bitch |
| Gambling | Miracle | Abandonment |
| "Calm down!" | Hypocrite | What if? |
| Forgiveness | Separation | Violation |
| Monster | Public speaking | Degrade |
| Betrayal | Sharks | Beast |
| Tattoos | Freedom | Grief |
| Purpose | Divorce | Aging |
| Favoritism | "Now, listen to me" | Politically correct |
| Repent | Guns | Trapped |
| Humble | Metaphysical | Pussy |
| Gratitude | Promiscuous | Shame |
| Anger | Jesus | Grandfather |
| Commitment | Greed | Grandmother |
| Frugal | Self-love | Profanity |
| Children | Stupid/dumb | Simple |
| Arrogance | Yesterday | Disease |
| Discernment | Compassion | "You should have…" |
| Naïve | Love | Recreational drugs |
| Retard | Evolve | Cheap |
| Don't | Naked/Nudity | Forgotten |
| Played | Public service | Praise |
| Control/controlling | Bad | Prescription drugs |
| Disappointment | Whip | Vulnerable |
| Independence | "We need to talk" | Lust |
| Adoption | Temple | "No" |
| Honor | Family | God/Universal |
| Useless | "Here, let me show you" | Power/Source |
| Ignored | Mama's boy | Lying/lies |
| Patriarchal | Victim | Adventure |
| Stubborn | Salvation | Sadness |
| Humiliation | Foreign cultures | Retired |
| Spanking | Unemployment | Dick |
| Unconditional love | Happy | Cow |
| Feminism | Dominance | Gossip |

| | | |
|---|---|---|
| Faith | Politics/status quo | Deception |
| Surrender | Cousin | Claustrophobic |
| Drug dealer | Judgment | Sissy |
| Tithing | Incompetent | Nice |
| Uncle | Music | Provocative |
| Aunt | Rape | Pansy |
| Cancer | Less than | Fear |
| Two-faced | Time | Blame |
| Generosity | Know-it-all | Stingy |
| Order | Wealthy | Now |
| Sinful | Priesthood/priest | Old |
| Ashamed | Future | Bitterness |
| Loser | Smile | No. 1 |
| Liar | In the way | User |
| Alternative medicine | Backstabbing | Bullying |
| "Doesn't that feel good?" | Emotional | Drowning |
| Struggle | Vodka | Foster care |
| Suicide | Phobia | Credit cards |
| Poor | Boys' home | Bastard |
| Rules | Girls' home | Brother |
| Acceptance | Can't | Sister |
| Body image | Soul | Taxes |
| Regret | Sensitivity | "You need to…" |
| Amen | Motherhood | Uneducated |
| Teacher's pet | Fatherhood | Confidence |
| Whore | Jealous | Demons |
| War | Police | Single |
| Molestation | Strong | Hideous |
| Responsible | Ego | Quirky |
| Needy | Dependent | Domestic violence |
| Fuck | Cunt | Rejection |
| Faithful | Physical appearance | Coercion |
| Anxiety | Discipline | Childish |
| Fool | Worrywart | Nun |
| Hate | Values | Spirit |
| Puppet | Trash | Should |
| Submissive | Honesty | Blood |
| Laughter | Bishop | Selfish |
| Homosexuality | Abuse | Respect |

# EXERCISE

| | | |
|---|---|---|
| Bigotry/racism | Educated | Adopted |
| Intimacy | Reliable | Isolation |
| Lesbianism | Coward | Marijuana |
| Son | Violence | Evil |
| Daughter | Pedophile | Punishment |
| Irresponsible | Teacher | Mission/missionary |
| Murder | Fire | Resentment |
| Alcoholism | Worship | Letting go |
| Space | Sleazy | High maintenance |
| Heart | Success | Romantic love |
| Coworkers | Technology | Special |
| Horny | Fat | Competition |
| Weak | Confrontation | Capital punishment |
| Brand name clothing | Smart | Cocaine |
| Clingy | No-good | Ex relationships |
| Lazy | Dishonesty | Loneliness/being alone |
| Organized religion | The Devil/Satan | Men |
| Women | Force | "I'll kill you" |
| "You're not good enough" | "You'll never amount to anything" | Eww |
| Punk | | Imbecile |
| Idiot | Gross | Half-ass |
| Piece of shit | Worthless | Dense |
| Daddy's girl | Chicken | "You're not worth it" |
| Goodbye | Cockroach | Stuck |
| Creepy | Prick | Tits |
| Second place | Stalker | Jackass |
| Witch | Screaming | "Go fuck yourself" |
| Heights | Cocksucker | Garbage |
| "I love you" | Handicapped | "I hate you" |
| Bald | Clowns | Impotent |
| Church | Obsessive | Beautiful |
| STDs (Sexually Transmitted Diseases) | Believe | "Stop it!" |
| | "Please" | Lame |
| Authority | Bankruptcy | Impossible |
| Homeless | Dumped | Lost |
| "I want you" | The holiday season | Baby |
| Filthy | Survive | Sorry |
| Hospital | Kidnapping | "It's your fault" |
| Delinquent | Dreams | Fired |

"Through the doorway of trauma compassion arose, blooming in my heart. Love. Simply love."

The following pages are designed to guide the reader in identifying emotional chaos attached to words and/or phrases. Self-empowering ourselves by discovering the Light within each experience – and rewiring our perception and letting go of what doesn't serve us – is a release of an old belief system and an embracing of a new belief system. Please take your time to uncover what lies beneath the surface of each word and/or phrase.

# Word: _____

## What feelings does this word or phrase emotionally unearth within me?

EXERCISE

# Word: _____

**Is this perception negatively affecting me? If yes, in what ways?**

# Word: _____

## How have I grown on a soul level by having the experience(s) attached to this word or phrase?

_____
_____
_____
_____
_____
_____
_____
_____
_____
_____
_____
_____
_____
_____
_____
_____
_____
_____
_____

EXERCISE

# Word: _____

**Shift it! My old programming and negative perception of this word/phrase no longer serves me. I embrace the growth of my character, the emotional growth of my being – the overall growth of my soul that has unfolded within me. My positive perception of this word/phrase is now…**

_____
_____
_____
_____
_____
_____
_____
_____
_____
_____
_____
_____
_____
_____
_____
_____
_____
_____

"Peace and contentment is a destination. You have to do the heart work to get there."

EXERCISE

# Word: _____

**What feelings does this word or phrase emotionally unearth within me?**

_____
_____
_____
_____
_____
_____
_____
_____
_____
_____
_____
_____
_____
_____
_____
_____
_____
_____
_____
_____
_____

# Word: _____

## Is this perception negatively affecting me? If yes, in what ways?

_____
_____
_____
_____
_____
_____
_____
_____
_____
_____
_____
_____
_____
_____
_____
_____
_____
_____
_____
_____
_____
_____

EXERCISE

# Word: _____

## How have I grown on a soul level by having the experience(s) attached to this word or phrase?

_____
_____
_____
_____
_____
_____
_____
_____
_____
_____
_____
_____
_____
_____
_____
_____
_____
_____
_____
_____

# Word: _____

**Shift it! My old programming and negative perception of this word/phrase no longer serves me. I embrace the growth of my character, the emotional growth of my being – the overall growth of my soul that has unfolded within me. My positive perception of this word/phrase is now...**

_____
_____
_____
_____
_____
_____
_____
_____
_____
_____
_____
_____
_____
_____
_____
_____
_____
_____

"Change your perception, transform your life."

# Word: _____

## What feelings does this word or phrase emotionally unearth within me?

_____
_____
_____
_____
_____
_____
_____
_____
_____
_____
_____
_____
_____
_____
_____
_____
_____

EXERCISE

# Word: _____

## Is this perception negatively affecting me? If yes, in what ways?

# Word: _____

## How have I grown on a soul level by having the experience(s) attached to this word or phrase?

_____

_____

_____

_____

_____

_____

_____

_____

_____

_____

_____

_____

_____

_____

_____

_____

_____

EXERCISE

# Word: _____

**Shift it! My old programming and negative perception of this word/phrase no longer serves me. I embrace the growth of my character, the emotional growth of my being – the overall growth of my soul that has unfolded within me. My positive perception of this word/phrase is now...**

_____
_____
_____
_____
_____
_____
_____
_____
_____
_____
_____
_____
_____
_____
_____
_____
_____

"Letting someone go doesn't mean we can't honor our feelings towards that person. If a person or situation is unhealthy, letting go is an act of self-love and a big step towards being happy."

EXERCISE

# Word: _____

**What feelings does this word or phrase emotionally unearth within me?**

_____
_____
_____
_____
_____
_____
_____
_____
_____
_____
_____
_____
_____
_____
_____
_____
_____
_____
_____
_____
_____
_____

# Word: _____

## Is this perception negatively affecting me? If yes, in what ways?

EXERCISE

# Word: _____

**How have I grown on a soul level by having the experience(s) attached to this word or phrase?**

_____
_____
_____
_____
_____
_____
_____
_____
_____
_____
_____
_____
_____
_____
_____
_____
_____
_____
_____
_____
_____
_____
_____

# Word: _____

**Shift it! My old programming and negative perception of this word/phrase no longer serves me. I embrace the growth of my character, the emotional growth of my being – the overall growth of my soul that has unfolded within me. My positive perception of this word/phrase is now…**

_____
_____
_____
_____
_____
_____
_____
_____
_____
_____
_____
_____
_____
_____
_____
_____

"Our perceptions become

our reality

but is it the truth?"

# Word: _____

## What feelings does this word or phrase emotionally unearth within me?

_____
_____
_____
_____
_____
_____
_____
_____
_____
_____
_____
_____
_____
_____
_____
_____
_____
_____
_____
_____
_____

EXERCISE

# Word: _____

## Is this perception negatively affecting me? If yes, in what ways?

# Word: _____

## How have I grown on a soul level by having the experience(s) attached to this word or phrase?

_____
_____
_____
_____
_____
_____
_____
_____
_____
_____
_____
_____
_____
_____
_____
_____
_____
_____
_____
_____

EXERCISE

# Word: _____

**Shift it! My old programming and negative perception of this word/phrase no longer serves me. I embrace the growth of my character, the emotional growth of my being – the overall growth of my soul that has unfolded within me. My positive perception of this word/phrase is now…**

_____
_____
_____
_____
_____
_____
_____
_____
_____
_____
_____
_____
_____
_____
_____
_____
_____
_____

EXERCISE

"Find beauty in the cracks. What appears broken is simply the Light finding its way out."

EXERCISE

# Word: _____

**What feelings does this word or phrase emotionally unearth within me?**

# Word: _____

## Is this perception negatively affecting me? If yes, in what ways?

EXERCISE

# Word: _____

**How have I grown on a soul level by having the experience(s) attached to this word or phrase?**

_____
_____
_____
_____
_____
_____
_____
_____
_____
_____
_____
_____
_____
_____
_____
_____
_____
_____

# Word: _____

**Shift it! My old programming and negative perception of this word/phrase no longer serves me. I embrace the growth of my character, the emotional growth of my being – the overall growth of my soul that has unfolded within me. My positive perception of this word/phrase is now…**

_____
_____
_____
_____
_____
_____
_____
_____
_____
_____
_____
_____
_____
_____
_____

"Sometimes the kindest word you can say to someone is "no.""

# Word: _____

## What feelings does this word or phrase emotionally unearth within me?

_____
_____
_____
_____
_____
_____
_____
_____
_____
_____
_____
_____
_____
_____
_____
_____
_____
_____

# Word: _____

## Is this perception negatively affecting me? If yes, in what ways?

_____
_____
_____
_____
_____
_____
_____
_____
_____
_____
_____
_____
_____
_____
_____
_____
_____
_____
_____
_____
_____
_____

**Word:** _____

**How have I grown on a soul level by having the experience(s) attached to this word or phrase?**

_____
_____
_____
_____
_____
_____
_____
_____
_____
_____
_____
_____
_____
_____
_____
_____
_____
_____
_____
_____
_____
_____
_____

EXERCISE

# Word: _____

**Shift it! My old programming and negative perception of this word/phrase no longer serves me. I embrace the growth of my character, the emotional growth of my being – the overall growth of my soul that has unfolded within me. My positive perception of this word/phrase is now...**

_____
_____
_____
_____
_____
_____
_____
_____
_____
_____
_____
_____
_____
_____
_____
_____
_____
_____
_____
_____
_____
_____

"Change can be scary but it's also exciting and holds unlimited possibilities. Open the door within you and hit the road of your heart."

EXERCISE

# Word: _____

**What feelings does this word or phrase emotionally unearth within me?**

_____
_____
_____
_____
_____
_____
_____
_____
_____
_____
_____
_____
_____
_____
_____
_____
_____
_____
_____
_____
_____
_____
_____
_____
_____

# Word: _____

## Is this perception negatively affecting me? If yes, in what ways?

EXERCISE

# Word: _____

## How have I grown on a soul level by having the experience(s) attached to this word or phrase?

_____
_____
_____
_____
_____
_____
_____
_____
_____
_____
_____
_____
_____
_____
_____
_____
_____
_____
_____
_____
_____
_____
_____
_____

# Word: _____

**Shift it! My old programming and negative perception of this word/phrase no longer serves me. I embrace the growth of my character, the emotional growth of my being – the overall growth of my soul that has unfolded within me. My positive perception of this word/phrase is now…**

_____
_____
_____
_____
_____
_____
_____
_____
_____
_____
_____
_____
_____
_____
_____
_____
_____
_____
_____
_____

"If your body is a vessel, then let your heart be the captain, and follow the light of your soul."

# Word: _____

## What feelings does this word or phrase emotionally unearth within me?

EXERCISE

# Word: _____

## Is this perception negatively affecting me? If yes, in what ways?

## Word: _____

### How have I grown on a soul level by having the experience(s) attached to this word or phrase?

EXERCISE

# Word: _____

**Shift it! My old programming and negative perception of this word/phrase no longer serves me. I embrace the growth of my character, the emotional growth of my being – the overall growth of my soul that has unfolded within me. My positive perception of this word/phrase is now...**

_____
_____
_____
_____
_____
_____
_____
_____
_____
_____
_____
_____
_____
_____
_____
_____
_____
_____
_____
_____

"Surrendering to love isn't weak; it's the power of God's compassion within us."

EXERCISE

# Word: _____

## What feelings does this word or phrase emotionally unearth within me?

_____
_____
_____
_____
_____
_____
_____
_____
_____
_____
_____
_____
_____
_____
_____
_____
_____
_____
_____
_____
_____
_____
_____
_____
_____

# Word: _____

## Is this perception negatively affecting me? If yes, in what ways?

EXERCISE

# Word: _____

# How have I grown on a soul level by having the experience(s) attached to this word or phrase?

_____
_____
_____
_____
_____
_____
_____
_____
_____
_____
_____
_____
_____
_____
_____
_____
_____
_____
_____
_____
_____
_____
_____
_____

## Word: _____

**Shift it! My old programming and negative perception of this word/phrase no longer serves me. I embrace the growth of my character, the emotional growth of my being – the overall growth of my soul that has unfolded within me. My positive perception of this word/phrase is now...**

_____
_____
_____
_____
_____
_____
_____
_____
_____
_____
_____
_____
_____
_____
_____
_____
_____
_____
_____
_____

"We hurt ourselves by internalizing projections. Let go of another's baggage and embrace inner peace."

# Word: _____

## What feelings does this word or phrase emotionally unearth within me?

EXERCISE

# Word: _____

## Is this perception negatively affecting me? If yes, in what ways?

# Word: _____

## How have I grown on a soul level by having the experience(s) attached to this word or phrase?

EXERCISE

# Word: _____

**Shift it! My old programming and negative perception of this word/phrase no longer serves me. I embrace the growth of my character, the emotional growth of my being – the overall growth of my soul that has unfolded within me. My positive perception of this word/phrase is now…**

_____
_____
_____
_____
_____
_____
_____
_____
_____
_____
_____
_____
_____
_____
_____
_____
_____
_____
_____
_____
_____

"Tears are the rain our soul seeds need to bloom."

EXERCISE

# Word: _____

## What feelings does this word or phrase emotionally unearth within me?

_____
_____
_____
_____
_____
_____
_____
_____
_____
_____
_____
_____
_____
_____
_____
_____
_____
_____
_____
_____
_____
_____
_____
_____
_____

**Word:** _____

**Is this perception negatively affecting me? If yes, in what ways?**

EXERCISE

# Word: _____

## How have I grown on a soul level by having the experience(s) attached to this word or phrase?

_____
_____
_____
_____
_____
_____
_____
_____
_____
_____
_____
_____
_____
_____
_____
_____
_____
_____
_____
_____
_____
_____
_____
_____
_____
_____
_____

# Word: _____

**Shift it! My old programming and negative perception of this word/phrase no longer serves me. I embrace the growth of my character, the emotional growth of my being – the overall growth of my soul that has unfolded within me. My positive perception of this word/phrase is now…**

_____
_____
_____
_____
_____
_____
_____
_____
_____
_____
_____
_____
_____
_____
_____
_____
_____
_____
_____

"We cannot control how another chooses to interpret our actions. Speak with integrity and follow the compass of your heart. Walk in a field of gold within yourself."

# Word: _____

## What feelings does this word or phrase emotionally unearth within me?

EXERCISE

# Word: _____

## Is this perception negatively affecting me? If yes, in what ways?

_____
_____
_____
_____
_____
_____
_____
_____
_____
_____
_____
_____
_____
_____
_____
_____
_____
_____
_____
_____
_____
_____
_____
_____
_____

# Word: _____

## How have I grown on a soul level by having the experience(s) attached to this word or phrase?

# Word: _____

**Shift it! My old programming and negative perception of this word/phrase no longer serves me. I embrace the growth of my character, the emotional growth of my being – the overall growth of my soul that has unfolded within me. My positive perception of this word/phrase is now…**

_____
_____
_____
_____
_____
_____
_____
_____
_____
_____
_____
_____
_____
_____
_____
_____
_____
_____
_____
_____
_____

"Every disappointment is an opportunity to reevaluate and maximize personal growth potential."

EXERCISE

# Word: _____

## What feelings does this word or phrase emotionally unearth within me?

# Word: _____

## Is this perception negatively affecting me? If yes, in what ways?

EXERCISE

# Word: _____

# How have I grown on a soul level by having the experience(s) attached to this word or phrase?

_____
_____
_____
_____
_____
_____
_____
_____
_____
_____
_____
_____
_____
_____
_____
_____
_____
_____
_____
_____
_____
_____

# Word: _____

**Shift it! My old programming and negative perception of this word/phrase no longer serves me. I embrace the growth of my character, the emotional growth of my being – the overall growth of my soul that has unfolded within me. My positive perception of this word/phrase is now…**

_____
_____
_____
_____
_____
_____
_____
_____
_____
_____
_____
_____
_____
_____
_____
_____
_____

"When people 'reject us,' maybe, in reality, they're holding up a beautiful mirror showing us how we've been rejecting ourselves. Maybe the heartbreak and the hurt in life is merely a roadmap to do our own soul work and create the love inside toward ourselves that we've been looking for in others."

# Word: _____

## What feelings does this word or phrase emotionally unearth within me?

_____
_____
_____
_____
_____
_____
_____
_____
_____
_____
_____
_____
_____
_____
_____
_____
_____
_____
_____
_____
_____

EXERCISE

# Word: _____

## Is this perception negatively affecting me? If yes, in what ways?

_____
_____
_____
_____
_____
_____
_____
_____
_____
_____
_____
_____
_____
_____
_____
_____
_____
_____
_____
_____
_____
_____
_____
_____

# Word: _____

## How have I grown on a soul level by having the experience(s) attached to this word or phrase?

_____
_____
_____
_____
_____
_____
_____
_____
_____
_____
_____
_____
_____
_____
_____
_____
_____
_____
_____
_____
_____
_____

EXERCISE

# Word: _____

**Shift it! My old programming and negative perception of this word/phrase no longer serves me. I embrace the growth of my character, the emotional growth of my being – the overall growth of my soul that has unfolded within me. My positive perception of this word/phrase is now…**

_____
_____
_____
_____
_____
_____
_____
_____
_____
_____
_____
_____
_____
_____
_____
_____
_____
_____
_____
_____
_____

"Choosing to uphold an illusion appears to be a shorter path but, in reality, it is a windy road giving the appearance of a shorter distance. Allow the Light of honesty and truth into your life and it shall Light up the place you seek within you."

EXERCISE

# Word: _____

## What feelings does this word or phrase emotionally unearth within me?

# Word: _____

## Is this perception negatively affecting me? If yes, in what ways?

EXERCISE

# Word: _____

## How have I grown on a soul level by having the experience(s) attached to this word or phrase?

# Word: _____

**Shift it! My old programming and negative perception of this word/phrase no longer serves me. I embrace the growth of my character, the emotional growth of my being – the overall growth of my soul that has unfolded within me. My positive perception of this word/phrase is now…**

_____
_____
_____
_____
_____
_____
_____
_____
_____
_____
_____
_____
_____
_____
_____
_____
_____
_____
_____

"Exploring perception is a spark in igniting the Light around and within us."

# Word: _____

## What feelings does this word or phrase emotionally unearth within me?

# Word: _____

## Is this perception negatively affecting me? If yes, in what ways?

# Word: _____

## How have I grown on a soul level by having the experience(s) attached to this word or phrase?

EXERCISE

# Word: _____

**Shift it! My old programming and negative perception of this word/phrase no longer serves me. I embrace the growth of my character, the emotional growth of my being – the overall growth of my soul that has unfolded within me. My positive perception of this word/phrase is now…**

_____
_____
_____
_____
_____
_____
_____
_____
_____
_____
_____
_____
_____
_____
_____
_____
_____
_____
_____
_____

"Love is your superpower."

# Word: _____

## What feelings does this word or phrase emotionally unearth within me?

**Word:** _____

**Is this perception negatively affecting me? If yes, in what ways?**

EXERCISE

# Word: _____

## How have I grown on a soul level by having the experience(s) attached to this word or phrase?

# Word: _____

**Shift it! My old programming and negative perception of this word/phrase no longer serves me. I embrace the growth of my character, the emotional growth of my being – the overall growth of my soul that has unfolded within me. My positive perception of this word/phrase is now…**

"What appears broken is simply beauty reorganizing itself into a new perspective. It's a shattered window to what was once trapped behind glass. Into the rays, blend."

# Word: _____

## What feelings does this word or phrase emotionally unearth within me?

EXERCISE

# Word: _____

## Is this perception negatively affecting me? If yes, in what ways?

# Word: _____

## How have I grown on a soul level by having the experience(s) attached to this word or phrase?

_____
_____
_____
_____
_____
_____
_____
_____
_____
_____
_____
_____
_____
_____
_____
_____
_____
_____
_____
_____
_____
_____
_____
_____

EXERCISE

## Word: _____

**Shift it! My old programming and negative perception of this word/phrase no longer serves me. I embrace the growth of my character, the emotional growth of my being – the overall growth of my soul that has unfolded within me. My positive perception of this word/phrase is now…**

_____
_____
_____
_____
_____
_____
_____
_____
_____
_____
_____
_____
_____
_____
_____
_____
_____
_____
_____
_____

"Have hope that people who hurt other people heal in themselves what drives them to hurt. Be grateful for the beautiful lesson they gifted. Let go with grace. Rise up out of the storm where it's quiet. Within your heart find a love so beautiful that sharing it is the only option. Be real. Be love."

EXERCISE

# Word: _____

## What feelings does this word or phrase emotionally unearth within me?

**Word:** _____

**Is this perception negatively affecting me? If yes, in what ways?**

EXERCISE

# Word: _____

## How have I grown on a soul level by having the experience(s) attached to this word or phrase?

_____
_____
_____
_____
_____
_____
_____
_____
_____
_____
_____
_____
_____
_____
_____
_____
_____
_____
_____
_____
_____
_____

# Word: _____

**Shift it! My old programming and negative perception of this word/phrase no longer serves me. I embrace the growth of my character, the emotional growth of my being – the overall growth of my soul that has unfolded within me. My positive perception of this word/phrase is now…**

_____
_____
_____
_____
_____
_____
_____
_____
_____
_____
_____
_____
_____
_____
_____
_____
_____
_____

"Lighten Up."

# Into the Integration

Recognizing negative patterns and owning how unhealthy choices and thoughts create grief is both enlightening and life-changing. Taking responsibility is the ultimate freedom. It lets us press "stop" on the victimhood movie continuously streaming on the screen of our minds.

During the integration process, we may question where one draws the line of responsibility. Are we responsible for another's hurtful actions?

People show us who they are, and if we pay attention, we can avoid a lot of the painful side streets we find ourselves traveling. Listening to that inner hunch; that gut feeling – our intuition – is a compass to joy. Hunches are our inner guidance system navigating us away from unhealthy situations that will cause emotional hurdles to jump over internally.

If we ignore our intuition and remain in an unhealthy environment, and/or keep people in our lives that disrespect our values and boundaries, we are inviting chaos into our being.

If we continue in negative thinking and continue making choices that do not benefit our happiness, we're contributing to the grief in our lives.

Old patterns play themselves out via people and their respective roles in our lives. Recognizing repeated patterns is a key to unlocking a new direction; it's a map to a new adventure our soul wants to explore.

On the other hand, while making "bad choices" can result in emotional suffering, they also afford beautiful opportunities for learning. Remember, each painful experience is a teacher.

Right now you are probably asking, so are mistakes truly mistakes? Is the pain we go through something to be celebrated? Well, yes and no.

> "Be the leaf on a tree. Sway in the wind and let Light filter through. Be the air for others to breathe and provide shade when they are tired. Go within to your roots and be grounded in the earth. Yet, be open to change and growth in new places. Die in the fall and come alive in the spring. Trust in the renewal and be still in just being."

Sadly, there are some experiences in life that could never be celebrated or thought of as a positive, per se; for example, childhood abuse or trauma in adulthood due to others or circumstances beyond our control (i.e. a superstorm that destroys our home). The emotional turmoil created from these uncontrollable circumstances can be a hard burden to carry.

That said, the same turmoil can be a catalyst for and even a roadmap to inner healing. It may require time, patience, forgiveness and gentleness. Be gentle with yourself and trust that letting go of the negative experience and embracing the hidden gift is exactly what your soul desires.

Don't carry bitterness around in your back pocket. Sometimes life lessons take time before settling within us. A new way of thinking and responding doesn't happen overnight. Emotions take time to sort out but finding the responsibility and/or finding the gem in the experience and letting go are a step in the direction of peace of mind.

Everything is a gift waiting to be unfolded.

"People will let you down. You know this. Yet, you continue hoping they will grant your greatest desire...

...But what you desire the most you already have. It's within you, waiting to be unfolded."

# The Dark Side of the Lily

We all have different shades to our personalities. Denying the darker shades of ourselves and presenting only our best sides to the world is like the false front building on a movie set. It sure looks pretty from the front, but it is flat and has no substance. It is just that – a front.

Why must one always present the best side of oneself and hide the undesirable parts? Why not own them, dissect them and understand how, with a little finagling, they can work to our benefit?

Accepting the darker shades of ourselves allows Light within to shine even more brightly. We all have positive and negative traits. No one's life is perfect. No one is perfect. We've all judged someone and been judged. We all lose our temper. We all have our good moments and our bad moments. None of us are one hundred percent consistent. Like the Universe, we're all expanding in some way on our own journeys and at our own pace.

We're made of Light, yet in the darkness we seek the Light. In that sense, maybe the darkness isn't to be feared; maybe the darkness is simply a key to finding direction to the Light. Maybe the Light within us is found by walking through the darkness that resides inside of us and then carrying a little bit of that darkness on our journey so that Light shines continuously. Embrace the challenging experiences of life for they are teaching you and unfolding the

> "A cloud sometimes provides shade. Other times rain. It's beautiful just being. Kind of like you. Accept all parts of yourself as a part of the beautiful whole."

Light within you.

Through the nourishing water of a stormy black cloud and beneath the rays of a bright sun, a lily sprouts forth from the dark soil into the higher planes above it. Part of that upward movement toward the sunlight is embracing the fact that dirt sometimes sticks, but in its gritty grasp, there is nourishment for the journey.

Strive for kindness and believe in the goodness of love, but don't be afraid of the natural "darkness" – ours or others. Life is a journey and each of us plays a part in the greater whole.

Our dimension is a hall of learning. The adversity we offer one another is a give and take. There is an element of giving and receiving via the moonlit path. Like plants, we thrive in the Light only and with moments of darkness. We can't grow without the inky aspects of our being – and someone else's – guiding us.

There is a reason why both Light and dark are present in our personalities. There is a reason everything has its opposite, including the Light and the dark within us. It serves a purpose. For without a little black seed and dark soil, there would be no flower; there would be no fruit.

On a spiritual level, maybe the seeds for growth were deliberately planted. And if everything in nature ties together in order to flourish, explore the possibility that this concept may apply to the inner workings of oneself as well.

Life is our healer. Trust that all experiences are designed to serve the expansion of the soul.

> "Life is our healer."

"Illusions appear real. The trick to breaking an illusion is seeing through it into one's reality."

# You Are the Creator

Who are we? Are we our patchy history, or do we have the ability to create a new tapestry of gold?

We are the creators of our lives. We are the miracle in our lives. Trust, let go, surrender to the pain and embrace the beauty of growth. The past is over, the future is unwritten, and the present is in our hands.

In life, we give our power away by waiting for a rescue. No one is going to rescue us; we rescue ourselves. Embrace the inner oracle and create your life experience.

Nurture the quiet within, still the mind, trust the process, let go and fall into the greatest love within your own soul.

> "Like a well-written recipe, she created her life. But the lack of spontaneity is the forgotten spice that dolls up a dish. She started seeing people and opportunities as doorways instead of destinations. She let go and tried new avenues. Life never tasted so good."

"Imagine the Universe as a backboard, and the energy you express as a ball. Just like a ball to a backboard, what we throw out energetically is exactly what comes back to us. Take notice of the negative people, experiences and patterns of grief in your life. These patterns are a reflection of what you've energetically "thrown" out; it's the unresolved pain and a false belief system within that is in need of healing. The key to changing the patterns - 'the reflections' - is changing our perspective of self. It's a process of understanding our current belief system and how it's either hindering or advancing us in our personal joy. Focusing on another person as the problem isn't the answer. Our reaction is merely a reflection of what's within us that needs healing. Following the reflection, going within, taking responsibility, and changing ourselves is a key to everything."

"Be the Light."

# Joyful Creation

There are times when we find ourselves in conflict with our thoughts and emotions. Situations don't always work out the way we hope, and another's actions can leave us emotionally traumatized and/or stuck in a negative state of mind. From our perspective, we've been wronged, and in this mindset, it's hard to consider another alternative.

Some of us may be fortunate enough to receive an apology, and we're able to build our confidence, let go of any grudges we may hold, and move forward. But painful situations, where no apology is extended, leave us picking up the pieces with our emotions in turmoil. How we choose to perceive a situation determines how our thoughts align. Positive thinking makes a difference in our attitude and births inner peace, joy, and happiness.

> "In detachment there is an inner stillness and a heart open to love."

When we're willing to step outside of our emotions and open our perception to a new direction in thinking, possibilities for joy become endless, and a previously unknown frontier in our mind appears waiting to be explored. We loosen our grip on "being right," and open ourselves to acknowledging the formation of the endless creativity. Realizing we have control over how we think opens a doorway to a new way of experiencing life, experiencing people, evolving ourselves and living in a state of joy.

We come to understand that how we perceive our circumstances impacts our joy, and we can then take responsibility for how we greet each challenge. This becomes a game changer in our reactions and interactions with others. Breaking down the barriers within ourselves is the first step to building a new foundation based in love.

Each of us has a belief system that determines what we perceive to be right or wrong. We're reared in a way that builds a thought process, and we navigate life through this structure. Usually, our belief systems are taught to us as children by our parents, teachers, friends, and, of course, our experiences. The trouble with belief systems is that they can be chains holding us in a prison of emotional pain.

Imagine a belief system as a pair of eyeglasses. How one sees the world is visualized through our spectacles. Everyone wears eyeglasses, and none are exactly alike. These eyeglasses have been handed down through the generations. Some eyeglasses have become outdated. The lenses are cloudy, and peering over the edge of the eyeglass lenses to see the world through one's own eyes is similar to the action necessary to create a new belief system.

Questioning one's reality is the way to think outside the box. Are we our bodies? Are we our earthly identities? Do our jobs and wealth define our value? Or are we more than our bodies, and more than the cars we drive, and more than our physical attributes and the sum of our life experiences?

If we're more than our bodies, then what are we? And if we're more than our bodies, then do the things – positive and negative – that we currently hold onto or value lose their worth? Seeing beyond the physical opens up a highway to the Divine, intertwined in countless beautiful moments.

When we turn that Divine eye inward, we see beyond our physical bodies and into the emotional dimension of our inner being. Hidden beneath our earthly cloak lies the Light of the soul. This Light is the Universal Power that binds us and it is the love of Spirit that connects every living being.

> "Dishonesty is simply someone else's inability to get real with themselves."

We can will the Light to come forward, and within that sacred, spiritual space, the physical falls away. Some find this peace through meditation. Joy bubbles up as attachments fall away. In the space beyond the physical, one can feel like a leaf on a tree swaying in the wind, and simultaneously feel like sunlight filtering through the tree's branches.

> "See everything through the Light. Become your soul observing the illusions of the mind.

With detachment to the physical and mental sphere comes true happiness. The emotional turmoil of the physical life falls away and a blending with the spiritual realm happens. Peace rises, and love and joy come to dwell within the physical vessel where the soul resides.

If we're not our minds and our bodies, then how can the grievances of life have true meaning? Are these disputes and disagreements based in reality at all? By the truth of the Light within, we find that blame has no meaning other than to teach us, and through sacred detachment the Light will prevail.

This sacred space can be elusive and requires practice to maintain, but it's a road within that is based on the fundamentals of our choosing. We can decide the way we perceive life and how we understand every experience determines the level of our joy.

Finding joy in detachment may seem like a counterintuitive route, but stepping away from an old pattern of thinking and perusing the opportunity of personal growth in every situation can be akin to removing constrictive shoes and wriggling one's toes in warm sand.

Emotional pain can feel like rocks carried around in our boots. Weighing us down, their burden is heavy and for some moving forward becomes impossible. Thus, when trapped in our own pain, self-pity steps forward and our joy can become squashed between anger, resentment and a big dollop of fear.

Living a joyful life is a choice; it means surrendering to the Universal Power within us. Seeing life in a black-and-white manner makes experiencing rainbows impossible. Just like settling under a fluffy blanket on a soft couch to watch the rain outside a window, observing sorrow as separate from us, like the raindrops on the windowpane, can be wonderful.

> "If one believes they're a spiritual being having a human experience, then why let anything manmade hold such value? Learn to separate from judgment and see from the heart."

Love is a white fire within us all, and by its illumination we can warm our souls. Beyond the illusion of the physical body dwells our soul, and beyond the soul is a Universal Spiritual Power that connects us. That power is a creative strength each of us can tap into at any time. Embracing ourselves as the designer in our lives is a new way of thinking that can open doors we previously couldn't perceive.

Like a flower closing to the moon and blooming to the sun, we thrive in Light. Difficult experiences can be vessels rocketing us to a higher vibration. When acting as creators, we can blend into the white Light within and send that Light outward. It is a choice to bloom or to wither.

Letting go of painful offenses can feel impossible, but if we dig into that pain and plant new seeds of thought, a forest of possibility awaits us. Offenses can feel personal, and it's common to internalize another's projection. If we look deeper, however, we find that what we project out is reflected back, and what we consider a grievance can become a map to personal healing. It's our responsibility to gaze into the Light of our own soul, find healing, and view the world through the perspective of love we are all composed of. Learning to tap into our creative power and dwell in the space of love is the key to living a joyful life.

How do we create joy? By choosing our thoughts in a way that builds a bridge to inner happiness. Like soiled clothes we remove from our bodies, it is our responsibility to remove negative thoughts from our mind. Holding onto anything that does not positively serve us is equivalent to taking a bath in a mud puddle.

It is the individual's responsibility to siphon nutrients from the dirt of negative experiences. They are our gifts of grief. But simply removing a person from our lives doesn't always eliminate the negative emotions, and some situations make it impossible to remove an offender. Chaos may arise. Carrying negative memories in our mind is equivalent to sipping a flask filled with poison.

If possible, remove negative individuals from your circle of friends and family. We may have to break up with someone who causes disruption to our harmony. We may have to shut the door on family members. Physically removing negativity is a positive action. Afterward, mentally place them in a beautiful land created in one's imagination and close the door.

Dealing with other people in our lives may require more complicated decisions. Perhaps we share a child or we have a negative co-worker or a bullying classmate, or are in an unhealthy relationship and cannot extricate ourselves from the situation in the near future. It doesn't serve us to focus on a negative situation we cannot immediately change. When forced into an unhappy environment, it is better to keep our thoughts positive until we can change our circumstances.

> "People in our lives change like the seasons. Some are annual blooms coming back to bring us color. Others are temporary bursts of color and then they go. Flow with the change and allow it to be as it was designed to serve you."

> "There will be challenges in life. Sometimes the 'dark' events feel overpowering and we may feel hopeless in situations that are painful. It may feel that another took our power away. Hope and strength can be found within us where an infinite amount of Light shines. And in that Light is a love so powerful waiting to be embraced. Our power cannot be taken away. Our love, our Light cannot be extinguished."

In either situation above, maintaining a positive focal point is essential. Divine Light exists in every soul. Discovering the Light within another in a way that allows our own soul to bloom yields many benefits, including a positive mindset. Seek the good in an individual and hold that viewpoint steady in your mind and heart.

We are all born creators. The people in our lives are actors in our personal play, just as we are actors in theirs. For individuals who have caused us grief, it may be easy finding a happy memory to replace the sorrow that lingers. And, when finding an immediate resolution to a conflict seems impossible, invent one. Use your imagination and make a positive memory. Use that memory as the blueprint for any person who has committed what you may consider an offense against you.

The last step is mental training. We must train our minds to focus on the positive memory we have attached to this person. That should be the only event we allow into our minds.

The people we have removed from our environment can no longer inflict pain unless we give them that power. It is through the use of our mind that we hurt ourselves, so we should master our thoughts in order to practice the attributes of a strong character. When unhappy ideas float up into your consciousness, turn your thoughts instead to the positive concepts you have put in place there.

For those people and experiences who remain in our physical surroundings, we can expect challenges; the key is to train the mind and focus on a positive attribute of the offender, and when in their company, detach from the present to instead enter into that positive world of your creation. The mind can be a powerful creator of beauty, and a haven for it!

This technique isn't an act of denial. The offense against you happened; it hurt, and it is what it is. For some, it's still occurring. Some environments are beyond our ability to change, but we can change our reaction to them. The fact remains that there are people in our lives that have caused and currently cause us pain. But the bigger reality is that we're spiritual beings having a human experience, which makes this world illusory, so the answer is to rise above our grievances and invite in joy.

Holding onto a painful memory or stewing in emotional torment doesn't serve us. Removing the cause of our pain, whether physical or emotional, finding the lesson it brings, integrating it into our lives, letting that experience help us grow and then releasing the negativity while moving forward in a positive mindset keeps us in a process of joyous expansion.

We are not only our bodies; we are instead beings of Light that are composed of love. Reaching for the Light within another via a perfect blend of detachment and love makes for a rising of joy and Light. Be in the world but not of it, and trust in the folding and unfolding of your own Light.

> "Reach for the Light in every experience."

"A tree sheds its bark as its trunk grows. Evolving and allowing ourselves to change is a process. Expansion is an ever-changing experience of the mind and heart, a recreating of ourselves as we blossom and grow."

"You are the creator."

# Personal note from author:

I hope you've enjoyed this workbook and that it has enriched your life in the same way it has enriched mine. The wisdom of the soul is available to everyone willing to tap into the power of their own inner being.

Our lives are a tapestry of beauty and pain. Each experience is a white, gold and black thread woven tightly together to create a pathway toward the Light.

Evil is simply the word **live** spelled backward. And all the suffering we see around us, suffering we deem "evil," is simply part of the third dimensional world we currently live in. No one can escape another's free will because life is a play of words and actions, but it's how we choose to evolve each experience to build our character – our souls – that is the golden thread.

Each of us is on a journey to expand the soul and learn from this world on a physical and emotional level. Living life asleep, unaware of how we're holding ourselves back and caught up in personal grief, is a vicious cycle. The journey within is the greatest adventure waiting to be taken. Everything we're looking for is within us.

Just like in a dream – when one falls asleep and does not realize it's a dream until they wake up – some people on this human-soul journey do not realize, until their death and the crossing back through the veil, the brilliance of their own Light.

A spiritual awakening, however, is like *lucid* dreaming, when the person knows they're within a dream and start creating from that space. The veil of our births, the one that made us forget who we are, falls away and we begin to remember the love of Spirit; the magnificence of our own souls and the potential within our creation.

Our Divine Light is an internal golden lantern in a sometimes dark and often challenging world. Going on an inner journey is the doorway to an awakening of our true nature, an igniting of the Light within us.

Transformational healing is remembering the magnificent beings we are; that we always have been; and that we always will be, and how we've been letting life's grief hold us back. And in that knowledge and release there is joy and creation of more Light. Shining a light inward shines a light outward, and, like a beacon of light, we become living lanterns.

Fire is often feared and viewed as destructive, but, for the Giant Sequoia tree in Northern California, fire is necessary. In the heat of fire, the cones of the giant tree open and drop seeds for massive expansion. Like a phoenix rising from the ashes, the seedlings reach for the light. Upward the trees grow, developing, and grounding in the womb of Mother Earth.

Being hurt and feeling the pain in life can feel like a burning fire inside us. Trust and fall into the feeling knowing that like the magnificent ancient trees, all is as it should be, and we are rising to the Light within us and blending into the Light around us.

It is my hope you too find comfort knowing that we are all on a massive soul journey, and no one gets out of this experience without making grand "mistakes" or experiencing pain while on this human adventure. *It's how we choose to bend those experiences to catapult us into the expansion of the Universe within ourselves that counts.*

Life can be tough for sure and sometimes we may want to throw in the towel, but our power and Light never goes out; *we* dim it. The good news is that turning up the Light takes just a shift in perspective.

For me, that shift meant embracing the harder aspects of life as spiritual gifts rather than as burdens to carry. This became an unrolling of a Universal love within me, and an embracement of the Light of my soul.

The definition of my father's name (Felix) is happy. Perhaps his "faults" were a great spiritual service toward the unearthing of Light within me, and a gateway in discovering the power of my love and the magnificence of my soul. In a backward way, he helped me find happiness within my own Light. What a gift!

Letting the grief in life teach us and moving forward in our personal evolution, stronger, with new tools from soul growth and transformed by the gifts of grief is the key. Transformational healing is a restoration of the mind, body and spirit to the knowing and embracing of the Divine Self.

Reach for the Light in every experience and every person, because it is our birthright to shine. Life *is* beautiful and it is what we make of it. Walking in the Light is a choice.

I choose Light; I choose LOVE.

In love,

Alejandria Kate

# About the Author

Alejandria Kate is an inspired writer, author, and certified Mind, Body, Spirit Practitioner through the Sunlight Alliance Foundation. Writing has been a constant since the age of seven, when she began keeping a regular journal. It became a vessel for healing and facilitated her transformation from victim to joy advocate.

Alejandria is passionate about personal development and uplifting others. She draws inspiration from the beauty – both large and small – that she observes in the world around her and from the quiet moments connected with Spirit and her own soul. She also believes vulnerability is a strength and an open heart is a key to inner joy.

In 2012, Alejandria graduated from the Institute of Children's Literature, where she studied writing for children and young adults. She is currently continuing her studies at the Arthur Findlay College of psychic sciences at Stansted Hall in Stansted, England in development of her spiritual and psychic abilities.

In her personal time she writes poetry and children's books and raises money for American Tortoise Rescue. She loves flowers and visiting the Big Sur, California coastline.

It is Alejandria's hope that readers feel comforted and inspired after reading her books.

Alejandria can be reached through her website, www.alejandriakate.com, where she also maintains a regular blog.

# Other books by Alejandria Kate...

## The Lantern Fairy

This is the story of a young girl who gains self-confidence through the power of a positive belief in her own abilities. Gold Berry is a sensitive fairy who enters a flying competition only to realize she was already a winner.

Alejandria Kate wrote The Lantern Fairy with the hope that Gold Berry's story inspires children to embrace the light of their own soul and the power in a positive belief.

## How the Strawberry Got Its Seeds

This is a story of a young girl who learns self-worth by embracing the very "flaws" that make her beautiful. Strawella Berry is a spunky fairy that enters a singing competition only to realize winning doesn't feel so good when one has to pretend to be someone they are not.

Alejandria Kate wrote How the Strawberry Got Its Seeds with the hope that Strawella's story inspires children to celebrate being different as well as imparts courage and confidence to any child who has suffered self-esteem issues.

Coming soon...

## Bubble Trouble

### Author's Amazon Central Account
amazon.com/author/alejandriakate

### Instagram:
https://www.instagram.com/alejandriakate/

### Facebook:
https://www.facebook.com/AlejandriaKate/

### Website:
https://alejandriakate.com

Manufactured by Amazon.ca
Acheson, AB